Thoughts to Ins

GANDHI

GAJANAN KHERGAMKER

JAICO PUBLISHING HOUSE

Mumbai • Delhi • Bangalore • Kolkata
Hyderabad • Chennai • Ahmedabad • Bhopal

Published by Jaico Publishing House
121 Mahatma Gandhi Road
Mumbai - 400 023
jaicopub@vsnl.com
www.jaicobooks.com

© Gajanan Khergamker

GANDHI
ISBN 81-7992-174-3

First Jaico Impression: 2003
Fourth Jaico Impression: 2006

Printed by
Rashmi Graphics, 31, New Islam Mills Compound, Currey Road (E)
Mumbai - 400 012 • E-mail: tiwarijp@vsnl.net

INTRODUCTION

Mohandas Karamchand Gandhi was born in Porbandar in Gujarat on October 2, 1869. From schooling in nearby Rajkot, he went to London to study law and later to South Africa where he toiled to improve the lot of immigrant Indians. He came back to India in 1915 and fought for her Independence armed solely with *Satyagraha,* non-violence and a phenomenal sense of conviction.

It was with sheer simplicity and conviction that Mahatma Gandhi had millions of Indians pooling their faith, even laying down their lives in pursuit of a dream — for India's Independence.

In January 1948, Mahatma Gandhi was killed by an assassin when he walked through a crowded garden in New Delhi for his evening prayers.

On The Soul

Gandhi

Anything which is a hindrance to the fight of the soul is a delusion and a snare, even like the body which often does hinder you in the path of salvation.

The soul that is hidden beneath this earthly crust is one and the same for all men and women belonging to all climes.

In the attitude of silence the soul finds the path in a clearer light, and what is elusive and deceptive resolves itself into crystal clearness.

The force of spirit is ever progressive and endless. Its full expression makes it unconquerable in the world.

3

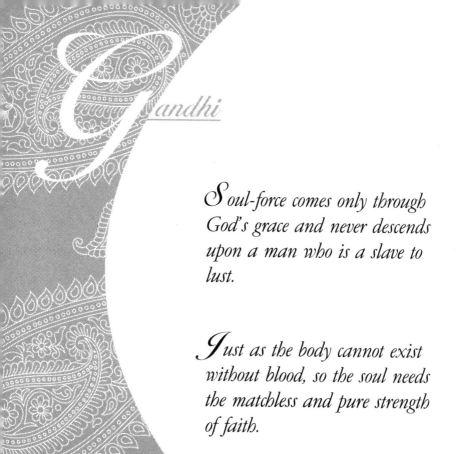

Gandhi

Soul-force comes only through God's grace and never descends upon a man who is a slave to lust.

Just as the body cannot exist without blood, so the soul needs the matchless and pure strength of faith.

4

On Faith

Gandhi

Faith gains in strength only when people are willing to lay down their lives for it.

Robust faith in oneself and brave trust of the opponent, so-called or real, is the best safeguard.

6

Every living faith must have within itself the power of rejuvenation if it is to live. Just as the body cannot exist without blood, so the soul needs matchless and pure strength of faith.

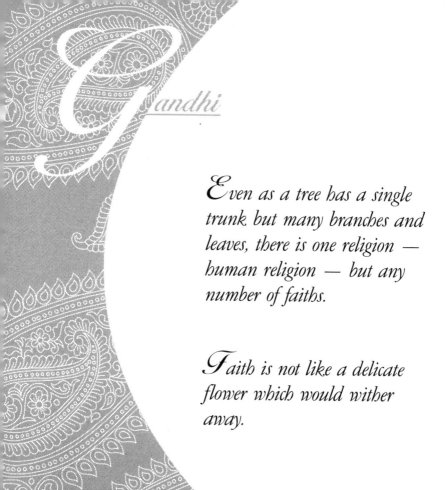

Gandhi

Even as a tree has a single trunk but many branches and leaves, there is one religion — human religion — but any number of faiths.

Faith is not like a delicate flower which would wither away.

8

*M*y effort should never be to
undermine another's faith but
to make him a better follower of
his own faith.

A living faith cannot be
manufactured by the rule of
[the] majority.

Gandhi

What is faith if it is not translated into action?

Faith is not imparted like secular subjects. It is given through the language of the heart.

On Truth

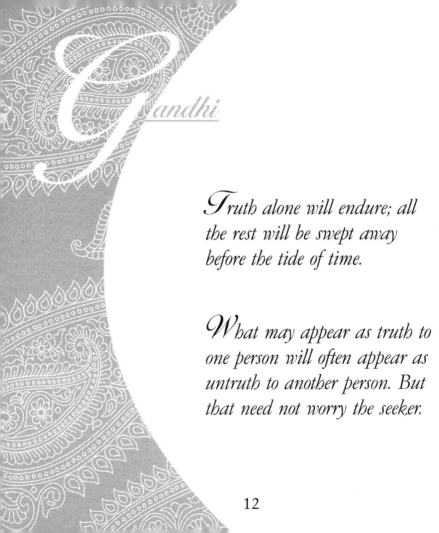

Gandhi

Truth alone will endure; all the rest will be swept away before the tide of time.

What may appear as truth to one person will often appear as untruth to another person. But that need not worry the seeker.

When I despair, I remember that all through history the way of truth and love has always won. There have been tyrants and murderers and for a time they seem invincible, but in the end, they always fall — think of it, always.

13

Use truth as your anvil, non-violence as your hammer and anything that does not stand the test when it is brought to the anvil of truth and hammered with non-violence, reject it.

Truth and untruth often co-exist; good and evil often are found together.

An error does not become truth by reason of multiplied propagation, nor does truth become error because nobody sees it.

Truth is the first to be sought for, and Beauty and Goodness will then be added unto you.

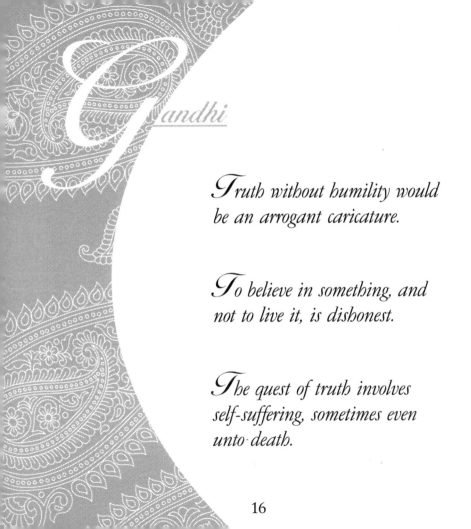

Gandhi

Truth without humility would be an arrogant caricature.

To believe in something, and not to live it, is dishonest.

The quest of truth involves self-suffering, sometimes even unto death.

On Satyagraha

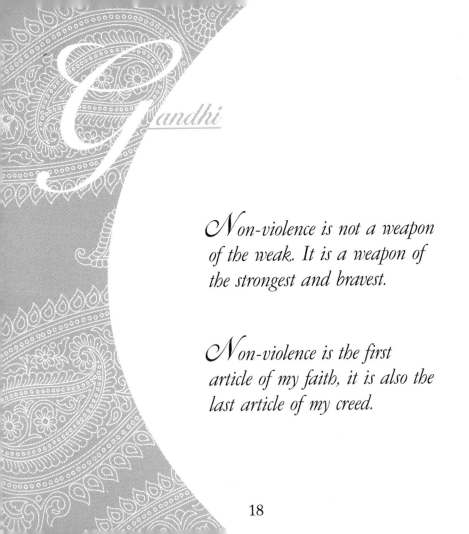

Gandhi

Non-violence is not a weapon of the weak. It is a weapon of the strongest and bravest.

Non-violence is the first article of my faith, it is also the last article of my creed.

The fight of Satyagraha is for the strong in spirit, not the doubter or the timid.

Satyagraha teaches us the art of living as well as dying.

My greatest weapon is mute prayer.

19

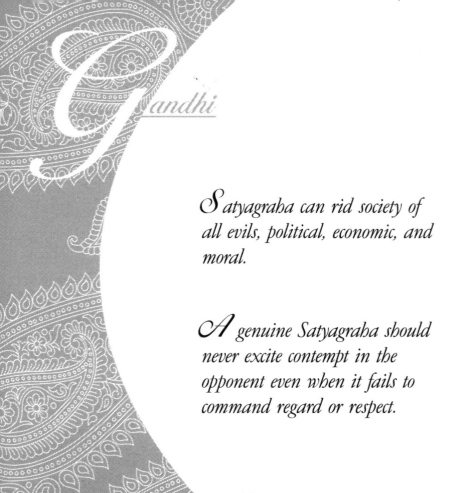

Satyagraha can rid society of all evils, political, economic, and moral.

A genuine Satyagraha should never excite contempt in the opponent even when it fails to command regard or respect.

Satyagraha thrives on repression till at last the repressor is tired and the object of Satyagraha is gained.

Satyagraha does not depend on the outside (for) help; it derives all its strength from within.

Gandhi

Satyagraha, of which civil-resistance is but a part, is to me the universal law of life.

For a Satyagraha brigade, only those are eligible who believe in ahimsa — non-violence and satya — truth.

On Violence

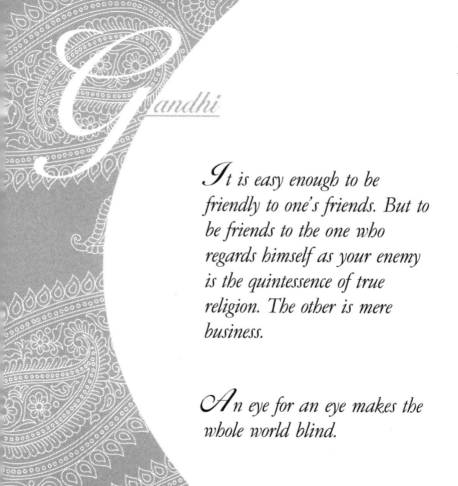

Gandhi

It is easy enough to be friendly to one's friends. But to be friends to the one who regards himself as your enemy is the quintessence of true religion. The other is mere business.

An eye for an eye makes the whole world blind.

24

Retaliation is counter-poison and poison breeds more poison. The nectar of Love alone can destroy the poison of hate.

I see neither bravery nor sacrifice in destroying life or property, for offense or defense.

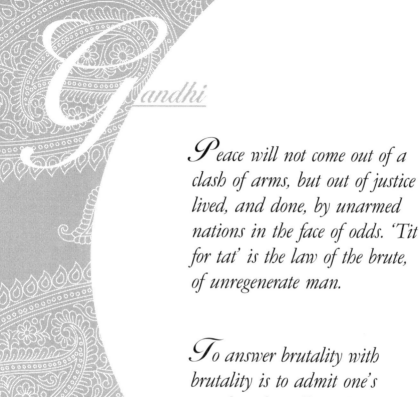

Gandhi

*P*eace will not come out of a clash of arms, but out of justice lived, and done, by unarmed nations in the face of odds. 'Tit for tat' is the law of the brute, of unregenerate man.

*T*o answer brutality with brutality is to admit one's moral and intellectual bankruptcy.

26

On Civil Disobedience

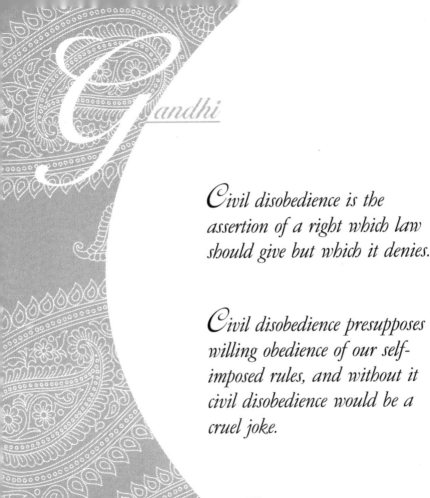

Gandhi

Civil disobedience is the assertion of a right which law should give but which it denies.

Civil disobedience presupposes willing obedience of our self-imposed rules, and without it civil disobedience would be a cruel joke.

28

Civil disobedience means capacity for unlimited suffering without the intoxicating excitement of killing.

Civil disobedience becomes a sacred duty when the State becomes lawless and corrupt.

29

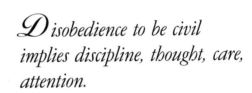

Gandhi

Disobedience to be civil implies discipline, thought, care, attention.

The only tyrant I accept in this world is the still voice within.

No co-operation with evil is as much a duty as cooperation with good.

30

On Vegetarianism

Gandhi

*I*t is very significant that some of the most thoughtful and cultured men are partisans of a pure vegetable diet.

I hold flesh-food to be unsuited to our species. We err in copying the lower animal world — if we are superior to it.

32

I refuse to buy from anybody anything, however nice or beautiful, if it interferes with my growth or injures those whom Nature has made my first care.

There is a great deal of truth to the idea that you will eventually become what you eat.

33

Gandhi

To my mind the life of a lamb is no less precious than that of a human being. I should be unwilling to take the life of a lamb for the sake of the human body.

I do not regard flesh-food as necessary for us at any stage and under any clime in which it is possible for human beings ordinarily to live.

34

On Freedom

Gandhi

No charter of freedom will be
worth looking at which does not
ensure the same measure of
freedom for the minorities as for
the majority.

The spirit of political and
international liberty is
universal and, it may even be
said, instinctive.

The attainment of freedom, whether for a man, a nation or the world, must be in exact proportion to the attainment of non-violence by each.

No government on earth can make men, who have realized freedom in their hearts, salute against their will.

Gandhi

No action which is not voluntary can be called moral. So long as we act like machines there can be no question of morality.

True non-violence should mean a complete freedom from ill-will and anger and hate and an overflowing love for all.

On Government

Gandhi

I look upon an increase in the power of the State with the greatest fear because, although while apparently doing good by minimizing exploitation, it does the greatest harm to mankind by destroying individuality which lies at the heart of all progress.

It is when the mass mind is unnaturally influenced by wicked men that the mass of mankind commit violence. But they forget it as they commit it because they return to their peaceful nature immediately the evil influence of the directing mind has been removed.

Gandhi

Government control gives rise to fraud, suppression of Truth, intensification of the black market and artificial scarcity. Above all, it unmans the people and deprives them of initiative, it undoes the teaching of self-help.

42

On Brahmins &
Brahminism

Gandhi

The Brahmin's duty is to look after the sanitation of the soul, the bhangi's that of the body of society.

A true Brahmin should be the very image of humility and not be proud of his knowledge or wisdom.

44

*W*here is the real Brahmin today, content with a bare living and giving all his time to study and teaching?

*B*rahmins are born, not so Brahminism. It is a quality open to be cultivated by the lowliest or the lowest among us.

45

Gandhi

I have the highest reverence for Brahminism, under which a class has been set apart from generation to generation for the exclusive pursuit of divine knowledge and consigned to voluntary poverty.

On Death

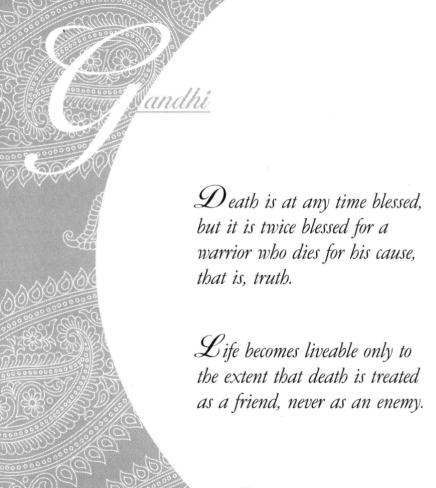

Gandhi

Death is at any time blessed, but it is twice blessed for a warrior who dies for his cause, that is, truth.

Life becomes liveable only to the extent that death is treated as a friend, never as an enemy.

*H*istory is replete with
instances of men who by dying
with courage and compassion
on their lips converted the hearts
of their violent opponents.

*I*t was the cowards who died
many times before their death.

Gandhi

Running away for fear of
death, leaving one's dear ones,
temples or music to take care of
themselves, is irreligion; it is
cowardice.

I came alone in this world, I
have walked alone in the valley
of the shadow of death, and I
shall quit alone when the time
comes.

50

*Y*ou may pluck out my eyes, but that cannot kill me. You may chop off my nose, but that will not kill me. But blast my belief in God, and I am dead.

*I*t is much more difficult to live for non-violence than to die for it.

51

Gandhi

It is as clear to me as daylight that life and death are but phases of the same thing, the reverse and obverse of the same coin.

Slow and inglorious self-imposed starvation among the starving masses is every time more heroic than the death of the scaffold under false exaltation.

On Education

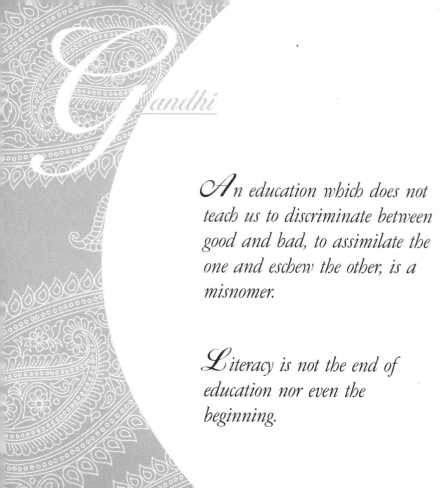

Gandhi

An education which does not teach us to discriminate between good and bad, to assimilate the one and eschew the other, is a misnomer.

Literacy is not the end of education nor even the beginning.

54

*B*asic education links the
children, whether of the cities or
the villages, to all that is best
and lasting in India.

*E*ducation in the
understanding of citizenship is
a short-term affair if we are
honest and earnest.

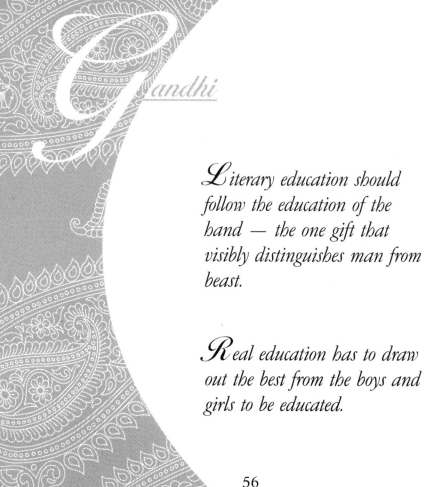

Gandhi

Literary education should follow the education of the hand — the one gift that visibly distinguishes man from beast.

Real education has to draw out the best from the boys and girls to be educated.

On Poverty

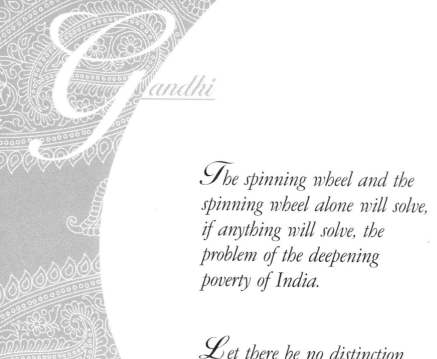

Gandhi

The spinning wheel and the
spinning wheel alone will solve,
if anything will solve, the
problem of the deepening
poverty of India.

Let there be no distinction
between rich and poor, high
and low.

58

To wear torn clothes is a sign of laziness and, therefore, of shame, but to wear patched clothes proclaims poverty or renunciation, and industry.

Unless all the discoveries that you make have the welfare of the poor as the end in view, all your workshops will be really no better than Satan's workshops.

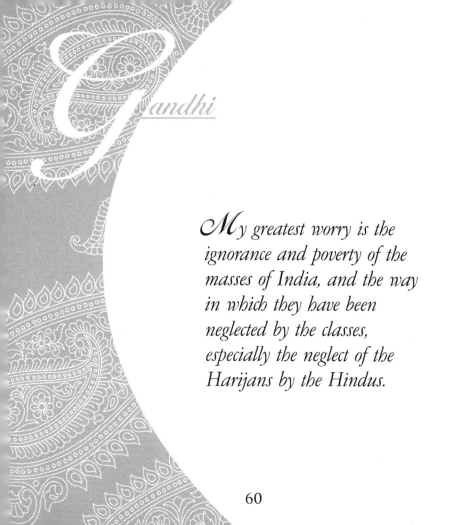

Gandhi

My greatest worry is the ignorance and poverty of the masses of India, and the way in which they have been neglected by the classes, especially the neglect of the Harijans by the Hindus.

On Swadeshi

Gandhi

True swadeshi is that alone in which all the processes through which cotton has to pass are carried out in the same village or town.

Swadeshism is not a cult of hatred. It is a doctrine of selfless service that has its roots in the purest ahimsa, i.e. love.

My nationalism is as broad as my swadeshi. I want India's rise so that the whole world may benefit.

I swear by swadeshi as it affords occasion for an ample exercise of all our faculties and as it tests every one of the millions of men and women, young and old.

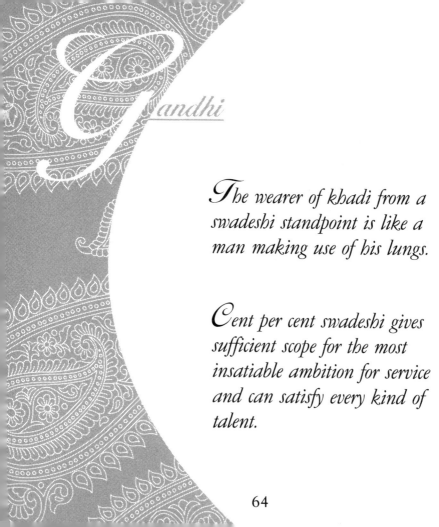

Gandhi

The wearer of khadi from a swadeshi standpoint is like a man making use of his lungs.

Cent per cent swadeshi gives sufficient scope for the most insatiable ambition for service and can satisfy every kind of talent.

On Suffering

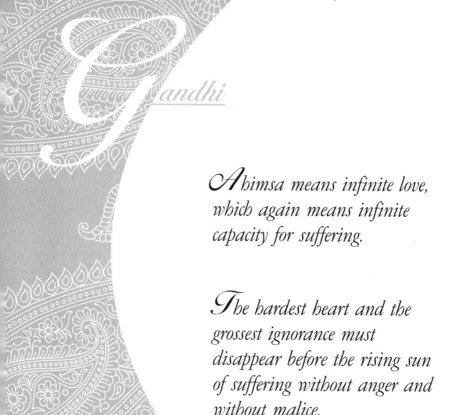

Ahimsa means infinite love, which again means infinite capacity for suffering.

The hardest heart and the grossest ignorance must disappear before the rising sun of suffering without anger and without malice.

True suffering does not know itself and never calculates.

Only the toad under the harrow knows where it pinches him.

The only way love punishes is by suffering.

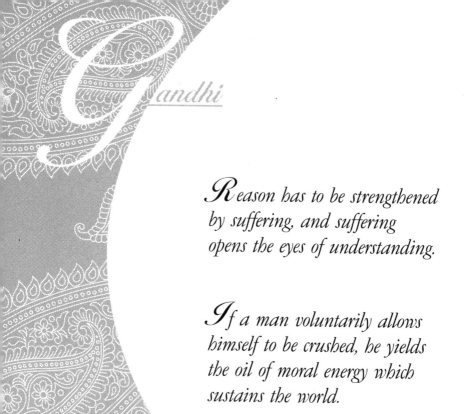

Gandhi

Reason has to be strengthened by suffering, and suffering opens the eyes of understanding.

If a man voluntarily allows himself to be crushed, he yields the oil of moral energy which sustains the world.

68

On Unity

Gandhi

I believe in advaita, I believe in the essential unity of man and for that matter of all that lives.

We are all leaves of a majestic tree whose trunk cannot be shaken off its roots, which are deep down in the bowels of earth.

On Wealth

Gandhi

Let there be no distinction between rich and poor, high and low. I own no property and yet I feel that I am perhaps the richest man in the world.

For every minute that I spin, there is in me the consciousness that I am adding to the nation's wealth.

On Cowardice

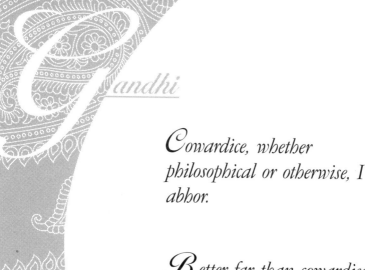

Gandhi

Cowardice, whether philosophical or otherwise, I abhor.

Better far than cowardice is killing and being killed in battle.

Cowardice is no sign of belief in God.

74

Could there be a greater proof of our cowardice than fighting amongst ourselves?

To change one's religion under the threat of force was no conversion, but rather cowardice.

There can be no friendship between cowards, or cowards and brave men.

75

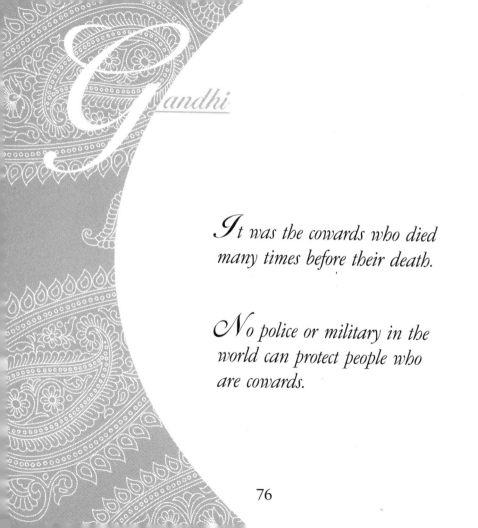

Gandhi

It was the cowards who died many times before their death.

No police or military in the world can protect people who are cowards.

On Law

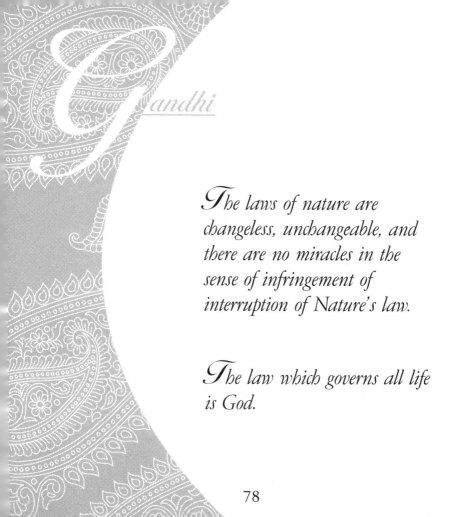

Gandhi

The laws of nature are changeless, unchangeable, and there are no miracles in the sense of infringement of interruption of Nature's law.

The law which governs all life is God.

78

The law and the Lawgiver are one. Affection cannot be manufactured or regulated by law.

The law is God. Anything attributed to Him is not a mere attribute.

Gandhi

*H*e is Truth, Love, Law and
a million things that human
ingenuity can name.

*W*here death without
resistance or death after
resistance is the only way,
neither party should think of
resorting to law-courts or help
from government.

On Marriage

Marriage is a matter of choice.

Marriage loses its sanctity when its purpose and highest use is conceived to be the satisfaction of the animal passion without contemplating the natural result of such satisfaction.

The privilege of marriage presupposes temperamental and other affinity.

Marriage is a natural thing in life and to consider it derogatory in any sense is wholly wrong.

83

Gandhi

Marriage is not an act of service. It is a comport man or a woman seeks for himself or herself.

Undefiled love between husband and wife takes one nearer God than any other love.

84